MW01174814

DUOLOGUE

ON CULTURE AND IDENTITY

Essay Series 15

ANTONIO D'ALFONSO
PASQUALE VERDICCHIO

DUOLOGUE

ON CULTURE AND IDENTITY

GUERNICA

Toronto·Buffalo·Lancaster (U.K.)

1998

Copyright © 1998, Antonio D'Alfonso, Pasquale Verdicchio,
and Guernica Editions Inc.
All rights reserved. The use of any part of this publication,
electronic, mechanical, photocopying, recording or otherwise
stored in a retrieval system, without the prior written consent of
the publisher is an infringement of the copyright law.
Printed in Canada.
Typeset by Selina, Toronto.

The Publisher acknowledges the support of
the Canada Council for the Arts for our publishing program.

Guernica Editions Inc.
P. O. Box 117, Station P, Toronto (ON), Canada M5S 26S
2250 Military Rd.,Tonawanda, N.Y. 14150-6000 U.S.A.
Gazelle, Falcon House, Queen Square, Lancaster LA1 1RN U.K.

Legal Deposit — Fourth Quarter
National Library of Canada
Library of Congress Cataloging Card Number: 97-74341
Canadian Cataloguing in Publication Data
D'Alfonso, Antonio, 1953-
Duologue : on culture and identity
(Essay series ; 15)
ISBN 1-55071-072-9

1. Canadian literature — Minority authors — History and
criticism. 2. Ethnicity in literature. I. Verdicchio, Pasquale, 1954-
II. Title. III. Series. Essay series (Toronto, Ont.) ; 15.
PS8027.D34 1998 C810.9'920693 C97-900786-0
PR9185.2.D34 1998

Overcome obstacles by force
Of love, do not knock them down, but loosen them
Like the action of water on soil.

Pier Paolo Pasolini

Is there enough love in our nation to back up a great moral advance?

Walter Rauschenbusch

I use the word "love" here not merely in the personal sense but as a state of being, or a state of grace — not in the infantile American sense of being made happy but in the tough and universal sense of quest and daring and growth.

James Baldwin

PASQUALE VERDICCHIO: Here, we are at the Roma Beach Café. We are drinking some nice Washington Merlot. It is about twelve years that we know each other. Almost exactly to the day. We first met in Rome in 1984 at a conference at the Canadian Cultural Institute . . . a conference on Italian Canadian immigration.

ANTONIO D'ALFONSO: It was a meeting of historians.

PV: Historians and sociologists.

AD: Organized by Roberto Perin. I remember you writing me, and my telling you we should meet in Rome. That you had to come, because you were going to be in Firenze anyway.

PV: I had written you after seeing some of your books, your book and Filippo Salvatore's book, at the Western Front in Vancouver. I said to myself, here are some Italians publishing in Canada. It was a revelation. And then I found your name in the Dust Books Catalogue of small presses, and I sent you some poems because I thought you were a magazine.

AD: Guernica was not a magazine, but, you are right, I did, in those days, have intentions of starting a *Guernica Review.* I really was serious about it. I wanted to do what these other people were doing in those days, which was to do small chapbooks of young writers. Smaller books than books, stapled pamphlets. It never really got off the ground, simply because I did not have the money. I never had money. Funny that you should be talking about books in a bookstore. I feel something has happened since. Our books are no longer in bookstores. It has been twelve years, and the cultural scene has totally changed. We find ourselves in La Jolla. I find myself discouraged in La Jolla because we cannot find our damn books in bookstores.

PV: That is a problem of distribution and cultural trends that . . .

AD: No. It is more than just the distribution. Something else is going on, which really bothers me.

PV: Nevertheless, since I wrote you, and you answered me to meet you in Rome, a lot has happened. Our books have reached out to certain places where they never would have without Guernica. You said . . . well, I am going to be in Rome, if you want to meet me, bring your work and meet me in Rome. So I came to Rome. I was living in Florence at the time.

AD: That's right. You were studying, no? What were you were doing? your Ph.D.?

PV: I was translating Antonio Porta's *Passenger*, the book that you eventually published.

AD: Is that when you translated his book? Amazing. Why did you start translating?

PV: I started translating as a way of learning English, a way of getting comfortable with English.

AD: Are you serious?

PV: Without any thought of actually ever publishing. The first book that I translated was by Antonio Porta, *Metropolis*. I went to Rome to this conference, and I was invited to read, which was very nice. You guys made space for me at the reading at Tor de Nona, the theater. Teatro Tor de Nona.

AD: My first "Italic" piece was published in Italy at that time, "Babel." A group of poets hosted us there, and then they printed a little pamphlet with a poem by Pier Giorgio Di Cicco, Antonino Mazza, and myself.

PV: That conference was very important for me, and I think it was for a lot of people. It was the first time that we actually met each other, all of us in one place. I had met Di Cicco in 1977 or '78 in Victoria, and actually interviewed him for a little journal there, *From an Island.* But he was the only one that I had actually met. I did not even know Dino Minni, who lived in Vancouver. Eventually, I met him through you. And Romano Perticarini. I didn't know him either, but eventually also met him in Vancouver.

AD: That was in May of 1984.

PV: We had some dinners around Rome. Afterwards you came to visit us in Florence . . . and we had dinners in Florence too.

AD: My life changed after that. It feels like my life always changes after I meet an Italian writer.

PV: It definitely represented an opening for me . . . finding a venue and interlocutors. On the way back to Canada, Liesbeth and I stopped in Montreal to visit you. We worked on my manuscript. You helped with the editing, and that was the beginning of *Moving Landscape.* Ironically, the year that I met you and everybody else and became a part of the Italian Canadian scene was also the year that I left Canada and moved to Los

Angeles. From Montreal we went to Vancouver, and then from Vancouver to Los Angeles.

AD: I find it strange that you should say that you began to translate in order to learn English, I consider you an English-language writer.

PV: I just did it to gain confidence, facility with the language (which, when some people see my poetry, they think I have yet to grasp). The first two books that I translated were Porta and then Caproni, around the same time, when I was still living in Victoria.

AD: Which we published many years after.

PV: Caproni Guernica published in 1990, that book had been done for eleven or twelve years. Just like Porta's *Metropolis*.

AD: You were the one who taught me Italian poetry.

PV: Those were, I think, some of the first Italian poets to be published in Canada.

AD: If not in America. They were never published in America until we took them there.

PV: But 1985 represents a beginning, starting with my book, and then A's book.

AD: That was a sad moment. I think it was my biggest hurt, as a publisher. I could not believe A. wanted to change his name to B. just before his book came out. There should be no question of nationality. It made his book totally obsolete the second it came out. Which is something that I found totally irresponsible for a writer. I am sorry to say that this difference of opinion created a friction between that writer and myself that has yet to be resolved. This was no isolated case, the disappointments to follow were many . . .

PV: With Italians?

AD: Publishing Italian writers outside of Italy is a disappointing experience. We do not read our colleagues' works. We do not take ourselves seriously enough.

PV: But you made your reputation with the French . . . the Quebecois.

AD: Yes, the Quebecois. Well, not only Quebecois. English Canadians as well.

PV: You had some Italian Canadians, but you branched out from Quebec.

AD: Gradually. What happened is that I wanted to produce more books in English, because if you produce only translations, you really have no one to promote those translated books. It is important that a writer promote his books. I really believe in that aspect of promotion, much like in the rock music system. You put out a record . . . you go on tour. The same is true for books. With translations, that process never occurs. The translator disappears. It is unfortunate. I am trying to change that. Desire for change was the idea behind the launch held in the month of January, 1996, when you came to Toronto with Irene Marchegiani Jones and Carol Lettieri. Toronto . . . Moving to Toronto was a very important moment for me as a publisher of translations, because, all of a sudden, our translations became alive.

PV: They become works.

AD: Yes. They become the personal works of these writers called translators. People are more willing than ever to buy books now. Yet it is very difficult to publish a book when there is no one to push it. Even when you have the big system behind you, you still have to be there, available to the reading public. If you do not make yourself available, who will do the promotion? I had to figure out ways of making money, and therefore, I started publishing Italians in a serious way. However, when I say "serious way" you must realize that there are not many Italians outside of Italy who write who are real writers, who write on a systematic basis. That is a major problem.

For example, though Filippo Salvatore is still an extremely active writer he has not published an English-language book since 1980. All his writing is done in French and Italian and it is all directed towards the founding of a renewed Canada. His courageous ideas have yet to be read by English Canada. The irony: here is a writer who is fighting for a united Canada in French Quebec and yet English Canada is perfectly unaware of his existence.

PV: Yet he is the one author that I saw in English Canada.

AD: But that was in 1980 and he has not published another English book since. He has published one play and a book of interviews on fascism in French. The rest of his stuff is in Italian. I remember sitting with him in front of a tape-recorder, recording the entire play, *La Fresque de Mussolini* with him, both of us acting each part in the play. That is how I was able to force words from him in order to put them on paper. I spend so much time pulling words out of potential writers. When did *your* book come out?

PV: 1985 was *Moving Landscape*; 1986 was *Passenger* by Antonio Porta. Soon in two years everything changed for me. I began to feel less invisible and that the potential for dialogue existed.

AD: The year I published *The Other Shore*, 1986, was a very bad year, because I did not have any books to publish. We were not writing

enough. A big problem. We speak a lot but we do
not write our ideas down on paper. I was hoping
to be able to force people to write. But that was
not the case. That is why I had to go to the
French in order to get books. This is how I started
publishing in French. By publishing in French, I
was able to find people who were more in the
writing tradition. You see, I do not think the Italian culture is a literary culture. I really think it is a
visual culture. The most prolific writers in those
days were Filippo Salvatore as a critic, but he did
it in Italian, so it was of no use to me, and Marco
Micone, who was a playwright. When I started
working with Fulvio Caccia he only had written a
few poems. He did have a book of poems, he had
made a commitment with another publisher. His
girlfriend of the time was working with a press.
All I was able to do was get a co-publication on
the deal. I could not have his second and third
books either. I had to wait for 1994 before I could
buy back all his rights and publish his Collected
Poems, *Aknos,* which won the Governor General's
Award.

On the English front, Pier Giorgio Di Cicco
was writing less and less until he eventually
stopped publishing completely. I really would
have liked to publish him, but he was publishing

left and right, which is not my idea of publishing. Mary di Michele and Frank Paci I knew I would never publish, because they, again, were distant realities entangled with other publishers who had more or less secured lifelong rights. The only writer I could have published on a regular basis, and I have, was Mary Melfi. That is it.

When you look at the other publishing houses in Quebec, it is very, very important that the publishing house publishes a group of writers. There are about fifteen writers who publish, easily, a book a year. That sort of commitment creates an incredible movement.

PV: You are talking about groups such as Les Herbes Rouges?

AD: Yes. They would do small chapbooks, and have one poem on a page . . . four liners . . . that would fill up a page, and a few poems would in the end fill up an entire chapbook. They would do these chapbooks regularly until they eventually became real books. By that time the authors had become famous and part of the mainstream and so it was time for them to put out real fat books, which they are now doing. This is a fine example of how marginal and often difficult writing takes over and displaces mainstream culture. I wanted to do something similar with *The Guernica Re-*

view, it was a way of making our presence felt, slowly, but regularly. But it was simply impossible to do: Marco Fraticelli, for example, writes a book of haiku every ten years. The quality was there but there was a real lack of outpour in the writing. I stopped thinking about movements and wanted first to remedy this serious and dangerous lack of writing. I did not know what to do. I finally had to go to Europe and publish French and Dutch writers in order to stay alive. I started doing Jean-Yves Reuzeau and Gerrit Bussink's anthologies because there was nothing being done in Canada that I could count on. I had no choice but to turn to Europe for help. Our community had few writers back then, and I believe we still do not have many writers. Am I wrong to say that many Italian Canadians are not committed writers?

PV: But you were also branching out in order to build your list. On the way it turned you into an international press, which is admirable and I would say unique, though unappreciated. As far as Italian Canadian writers, it is true. If you take a good hard look there are actually very few who do consistent work, who do it as their life's work.

AD: But there were mistakes, happy mistakes, you know, along the way. My whole goal was to publish . . . have a stable of writers, and grow all together. That is still my goal. Writers should work very closely with one publisher and vice versa.

PV: There is something about certain writers that stick with you and do not publish each new book with a different press. To become exclusively Guernica writers: that is more a way of doing that comes from elsewhere, which is not a North American practice. There is a lot of resistance to your practice from writers.

AD: That is because I do not think they are writers interested in culture. They are interested in business.

PV: I don't know . . . if I have a book, a manuscript that I have already given you, and I have another manuscript ready, and I have a press that wants to do it. Why should I not go to the other press? You must also consider a writer's anxiety and need to see something in print when it is done.

AD: When you do that, you divide an already small market of 500 buyers. One should not divide the market. It is counter-productive. Two poetry books will not find 500 readers in two different markets. Two poetry books will still find only 500 readers. In fact, those two books divide the possibility of selling 500 copies of one book into half. So you have one book that sells 250 copies and a second book that sells 250 copies. This sort of attitude encourages fights between writers and publishing houses. You turn them into enemies by fostering a false sense of competition where in reality there is no selling going on. The goal of any serious writer is to produce a body of work, and then ask your publisher to rent it out to a larger production outlet or get it translated. This is what I always want to do. Let's do a collected work and eventually rent it to a bigger press. If a writer publishes left and right it becomes very hard for a publisher to promote this writer's work. All the publisher will ever do is promote his own books. You cannot expect a publisher to promote the writer's books produced by other publishers. What is not in your publishing house does not exist. For instance, Guernica once published one writer who gave me Books 1 to 4 of a certain project she was working on. Unbeknownst to me that same year, she gave another press Books 6 to 8, and a third book, Book 5, went to a third press. What value was this to any one of the three presses? The exercise seemed futile. Because the books all came out at the same time I am sure she sold only a third of what she could have sold had she published the three books not simultaneously with three different presses but successively with one press. Do you think the three presses sold the books? We could not sell the book even if it was a good book. None of the other two publishers sold their books. In the end, did this venture make her more famous? Of course not. It might have helped her get tenure at some university, but it did not do anything else for her career as a writer. In fact, she has stopped publishing books altogether. She does not know which press to go to anymore. Such is the outcome of dividing one's work among different publishers. One day every publisher will slam his door on your face.

PV: As far as tenure goes, the pressure to publish pushes people to do this. But I don't know if it is that or, again, a writer's vanity.

AD: You are talking about tenure, not the world of writing, or *il fare cultura* (to make culture).

PV: Obviously, the pressure to publish for tenure pushes people to publish as much as possible. At the same time, I think that most writers do not really think in depth about the publishing aspect of writing. For a writer, the most important thing is to see your book out, and it does not matter where. Personally, I felt that same way for a long time. To me, the most important thing was: as soon as I have something, I want to get it out to a press. And if I had something with you, and I was waiting for my book to come out, I felt it was okay to go to somebody else with another manuscript. But I have changed my outlook. It has been slow, but I have changed my outlook on publishing, and it is probably the result of realizing that every press takes forever to do a book, no matter who it is. I have had the same experience with every press that I have dealt with. That it is not a matter of how many books you have out there, but how you present those books at your readings and elsewhere. And the importance of those books is in having people know them, and not just having them sit in warehouses.

AD: What is the use of having fifty books out there that sell twenty copies each, when you could have one book every three years that really makes people understand what it is that you are doing. When one is invited to do a reading it is fundamental to bring just one book. One reads from that one book, so that people can say, "Oh, I like it," and buy the book. This is the way to eventually exhaust the market. This is the goal of a book: it must exhaust its potential market. This is a lesson I learned from Gaston Miron. That is what I did for *The Other Shore*. I have been living off this one book since 1986, in English, French, and Italian. In between I did not feel the need to publish other books, simply because there was no need to do so until I got the message out about *The Other Shore*. Once that message became clear I was ready to embark on a different project which ultimately was linked in some way to *The Other Shore* which was, in turn, linked to *Black Tongue*. If one has a large book, it can take many years before it exhausts its literary and human experience. In the end every writer does but a single Collected Works to which one then adds other chapbooks done along the way and which finally give the entire project a new dimension to an author's vision.

PV: It takes a long time for a book to filter through. I do not have many reviews of any one of my books. I have some for each, but not many. So I feel that a lot of the real basic groundwork has yet to occur as far as my writing is concerned.

AD: I would not call those few words reviews. Are they really reviews?

PV: No, I do not think there are any real reviews.

AD: Exactly. How many people have done an in-depth analysis of your poems?

PV: I have never received any of those for any of my books. No one has written about any of my books in that way . . .

AD: How many books have you published?

PV: Books of poetry? Five books, and two chapbooks.

AD: They deserve a serious analysis.

PV: But I am finding that the people who are talking about my work, who are writing papers for school, are some young writers here in the U.S.A. I get calls about *Moving Landscape* and *Nomadic Trajectory,* especially *Nomadic Trajectory.* And *The Posthumous Poet.*

AD: How do you explain that?

PV: It takes a while for this material to filter to levels that people will find useful or find important. I have come to the realization that my work maybe is not important for Italian Canadian writers or Canadian writers, as far as that goes.

AD: When I speak of "they" I speak both of the Italian Canadian scholars, if there are any, and non-Italian Canadian scholars who reduce and funnel new writing into stereotypical analysis or stereotypical parameters of what a good poem should be. Right now, you do not qualify. You and people like Mary Melfi do not qualify in those categories. I mean, you both are the outcome of the culture. The conscious outcome of a conscious culture. Many people do not realize that your goal is the invention of a new poetic language.

PV: My experience with funding agencies such as the Canada Council or Multiculturalism has been exactly that. I have never received anything from the Canada Council except for a couple of reading fees and a travel reimbursement. Often, they have referred me to Multiculturalism which says that I do not represent the interests of the Department of Heritage Canada (Multiculturalism) under the parameters that have been set up as multicultural.

AD: These parameters are content based.

PV: They are content based and thematic. We know this is the most simplistic approach to any text. It is the most obvious. It could form the basis of more in-depth readings but it very rarely does. And there is a whole industry of critical writing that is based on this methodology that finds it useful to maintain and propagate it. It is also the most effective way to demote a work of literature, by reducing it to its mere themes and by keeping on presenting certain themes as the most representative ones of any one particular group, and that's that. It presents a very shallow and unidimensional picture of what any group or culture is capable of achieving and it is therefore effective in eventually dismissing their products as shallow and unidimensional. Unfortunately, I would say that some of our worst enemies as far as short-changing our work come from within our own group. Their reviews propagate a certain mediocrity at the level of criticism as well as the writers considered as being less than serious.

AD: Maybe you should do a cubist reconstruction out of a menu . . . an Italian Canadian menu?

PV: That would probably do it, huh? Remember how I used to recite menus at our conferences?

AD: Blaise Cendrars wrote poem-menus when he was starving. He wrote menus of all the possible meals he would like to have had but could not.

PV: It might sound like we're bitching about our visibility but, more than that, I find it interesting as a sociocultural phenomenon whereby critics prescribe ethnicities. You have to fall into this or that category or else. This attitude also is true of those who support so-called "official culture." We are the first ones who are guilty of reinforcing stereotypes. Because the only things that we will teach in courses or write about are those that best fulfill expectations.

AD: When you speak of stereotypes, you do not only imply content?

PV: No, no. I also mean form . . . the approach to presenting an argument. The conventional narrative form, for example, falls away from our cultural needs. If you want to look at our art and cultural history as a tradition, a linear narrative falls outside of that. Something that tells a story about an individual experience falls outside of the tradition. The oral tradition, if you like. The tradition we come from and the tradition that has been handed down to us. There is no linear narrative in a recipe. We are eating a plate of *amatriciana,* made in La Jolla by Roman people, recent arrivals from Rome.

What we eat in Rome might be different from this in one way or another. It is a recipe, a document. You might write it down, you might pass it on orally. There is no linearity. The only linearity is in some of the ingredients used, but not all of the ingredients. And so, I think by offering a nice, pat story of an individual experience, and presenting that as "the experience of a group," is leading everyone astray. We are not taking enough time to look at how each one takes that recipe and makes it individual.

AD: Maybe critics do not want to know that. Although to admit it is to give them a credibility which they lack altogether.

PV: We do not want to either blame them or give them too much credit.

AD: There is no attempt, by underground or mainstream culture, to take the Others seriously, on both the English and French side.

PV: That is true. It is not just the Italian Canadian critics. If you go outside of that group, it is not as though other people are noticing this writing. Only rarely is something that is not noticed by Italian Canadians noticed by someone else. Everyone is conditioned to expect something from so-called "ethnic" writers. Unless the expectation is fulfilled by the product, it will create yet another region of marginality within an already marginal cultural space. I have told you that a few people have approached me about my writing, people who are interested in what I'm doing with language and its structure. It is a small number of people, but these are people I respect. Fred Wah. For example, Daphne Marlatt and some young writers here in California. And, to me, that is important. A very small number, but it is not numbers that count, it is their approach to my work. They are interested in similar aspects of language and writing. Poetry is a medium for experimentation. Poetry is a laboratory, a linguistic and cultural laboratory, rather than a place to tell a story and only a story.

AD: That goes against what Dana Gioia says, that "poetry must be narrative."

PV: I do not agree with poetry being narrative at all as an over-riding requirement. Poetry contains narrative. It has moments of narrative. But those moments of narrative are also part of the imposition of language. You have to use a certain convention, and we follow that. If you look at my poetry, it is very fragmented, but there are moments of narrative. I fall into these moments of narrative that make connections. I do not believe that we think in linear narrative modes, and I think poetry reflects our way of thinking, our mode of thinking.

AD: My novel, *Fabrizio's Passion (Avril ou L'anti-passion)*, tells a story by the use of fragments.

PV: A very important novel.

AD: You keep on saying that. I do not know why. The Quebecois and the French liked it. The French really enjoyed it. A publisher from France wrote me, and would publish it only when the trilogy was completed. Whereas I was destroyed by English critics. They said I did not know how to write in English. That sort of attack hurts, because I am an English writer after all. But the English destroyed the novel because there was the lack of characterization. My novel tells a story, but not in a conventional way. Jean-Luc Godard said that to tell a story is the aim of all art. But that does not mean that it has to be a good story or that it has to be a story with a beginning, a middle, and an end. The elements of a story do not have to be there or placed in that order. You can have the end in the middle, and the beginning at the end, and the middle at the beginning. You can have no end or beginning at all.

PV: And they do not have to be present in the same book at the same time.

AD: Exactly. Where would they be?

PV: You can have the beginning in your head. You might be writing down the middle, and who knows when the end will materialize?

AD: That is true. In your case, I think you start with the end all the time. You do. Your poem in *Moving Landscape* about "Artaud and Nobody" is about the end of a culture.

PV: We are at the receiving end. That is why it is the end. But that end is also a generating end.

AD: I would go further. What I am trying to say is, I think the purpose of your writing is to describe the death of a culture . . . of some culture. That is why you are busy with reconstruction. The story comes later on in your writing. You are now finding a new voice, and it is becoming more narrative. I think *Nomadic Trajectory* and parts of *Approaches to Absence* certainly belong to the reconstruction of a language phase of your work. You said it yourself: you had to "learn" the language. I assume you mean at a symbolic level, right?

PV: Yes. But not only. Because I often feel inadequate at the level of vocabulary. So it is at the practical as well as the symbolic levels.

AD: Because, like I said, I think you are an English writer. But you are inventing a language that will fit your needs.

PV: Yes. Yes. A language that I may temporarily feel at ease in . . .

AD: That is exactly what I said or wanted to say about your work in my book of essays *In Italics*. That you have been totally stripped of your identity. I really believe what John Paul Sartre says when he speaks about the Jewish people. He says, "It is the other who invented the Jew, and if he didn't exist, the other would have invented him." The Jew has always been, in history, the one that has been stripped of the right to assimilate. But, in the meantime, he was able, thanks to the word, the written word, to reinvent narration that would talk about their culture. You are doing the same thing for the Italian peoples. You are doing exactly what the Nicole Brossard is doing for the French culture and women in French culture.

PV: You are doing the same thing in a different way. Mary Melfi is doing that. The writers that I've quoted in my critical writings have been writers that I find do the same thing. Not necessarily in the same way that I do it, but somewhere else along the spectrum of language. I came to Canada at an early age. I was around twelve. The English that I learned was a language that I needed to learn to get by day-to-day. But I felt it was not a language adequate for what I wanted to say. It did not represent me. As I grew older and started to learn more about Italian culture, I began to react to Italian as a standardized language. We have that in Italian culture constantly, day to day. Even in graduate school, you hear that the "only person who speaks proper Italian is the person who comes from Florence. Everyone else does not speak proper Italian." So we have that history in Italy. My activity, therefore, is aimed both at English and at standardized Italian. I am trying to find, not that I want to write in dialect, but I need to find a language in which I am able to express my condition. The condition is not unique, it is the condition for a lot of people who migrate from one place to another. I don't want to make it representative, but, for me, I needed to find a place, a position where I could start writing. I needed to start writing by removing all the excess that I thought was not useful to me. Along with that is the image of one's self in a foreign language.

AD: In many ways, you are still very Baroque, New Baroque.

PV: Yes. Because the infinite intricacies of language are Baroque.

AD: Because you have a problem with language, did it ever cross your mind that you could have been a painter? You are also a photographer.

PV: I would love to be a painter!

AD: I believe you would be a very fine painter. Have you ever tried seriously at working in another art form besides writing?

PV: No. I thought of going to art school at one time.

AD: Why did you not go?

PV: I have always wanted to be a visual artist but I thought that I should be doing something more useful, and become more professional and career-minded. I used to be into music and wanted to go to art school. One of my high school art teachers encouraged me. But then the hang-up of coming from my sort of socioeconomic background pushed me to university. I wasn't pressured to do it, but I felt that I should. Illiteracy is still a very close reality for us. Education is always something that had to take a back seat to more important survival strategies. I felt the necessity to make the leap beyond my parents' minimal elementary school education.

AD: You probably would have ended up painting like Italo Scanga. Scanga does with painting what you are doing with writing. If you look at the films made by Italian Americans, Italian Canadians, or the Italians from Italy, they are constantly searching for a language that is their own.

PV: Yes. And you did it with film.

AD: Well, no . . . I . . .

PV: Yes . . . Come on.

Italic culture

AD: I tried to make films, but to talk about my films would be misleading, since the films I did were failures. Maybe this is what is interesting about my films. The fact that there are failures. Truthfully, part of Italian culture can be referenced in my films. That is why I wanted to do film in the first place: I needed to express not only myself, but something else. I really feel that there is an aspect of Italic culture that can be captured by visual language alone. I use *Italic,* a term which I prefer to Italian, because when we speak about "Italian" culture everything becomes so ambiguous; besides, Italian is nationalistic. Italic culture, not Italian culture, is what all Italians in the world aspire to. It is one step higher in the spiral of culture. Did you know that Italian culture is going to die because there is a lack of Italians in the world?

Gaston Miron told me that once in Rome where we met. Gaston gave me beautiful poems that he had written while he stayed there. He spoke about how much he loved Rome. One evening during supper he spoke about a conference he attended in Italy in 1986 which had been organized by Unesco on world demographics.

The conclusion many countries arrived at was the following: for a culture to survive, it needed 150 million persons. If one did not have those numbers, that particular culture would slowly but surely disappear.

There are not at the present moment 150 million Italians in the world, so it is sad to conclude that the Italian culture is about to die. When I said this at a conference in New York, Italian Americans were shocked and quick to attack me. There is a story about an Italian writer who, when told "You should be proud to be representing Italy," replied: "Why should I be proud. I write in a dead language." It is awful to admit but it is the truth. Italian will one day be as dead as Latin. In spite of this tragic outcome, I still believe in the Italic cultures of the world. Italic cultures have gone through many phases in their history, they have spoken many languages, and still they are the same peoples. What remains goes beyond the limitations of language: what remains is the visual, the musical, the non-verbal aspects of the culture.

Music is an essential part of Italian culture. If you listen to Franco Battiato, who is a major composer, you get the impression that he is attempting to place Italian reality on a sphere of existence that no one has done before. It is this aspect of the non-linguistic world that led me to film. Film enables the Italic reality to come through non-verbal expression. Danny Allielo, Robert De Niro, Al Pacino, Nicholas Cage, and John Turturro are great Italic actors. At their best, what they express through the non-verbal is at once unique and universal. The message goes beyond the roles that they are portraying and lead us into the world of the individual in his small ethnic world. Personally, I really never had a chance to go deeply into film. I would have loved to, but it is so expensive to do films. Had I received in 1979 even $25,000, I would have been able to do the films I really wanted to do. To make a film one needs a lot of money and without money even the best idea becomes small and immature.

PV: It seems that we are going through a period in which many independent film makers seem to be finding it a little bit easier. And, as more film makers do that, they tend to support each other. So there is a network of film makers now that enables those things to happen a little bit more easily. We see ethnicity as something of value. We have our vision of what it might mean to be Italic. Once we come into a different culture, and we go into the Quebecois culture, or in my case in Vancouver, into a WASP culture, and now in the U.S.A., we maintain our ideals or ideas of what we are. Even though we are always told from the outside what we are, we obviously have our own idea of what we are, and we function on that, as a function to what is being told about us.

AD: What is the function of ethnicity? One side wants to uphold it, and the other side wants to break it down. Analysis of ethnicity reveals that any one person is given only one chance to assimilate. Once you've failed to assimilate, you are kicked out of the world you wanted to assimilate into. You are marked for life. If you're marked for life — there are many people who are marked for life — you have to persevere and not retreat into solitude. Many immigrants retreat into solitude which can make them prone to insanity. This is a theme that interests a film maker friend of mine, Nicholas Zavaglia. And I agree with him totally.

PV: The high incidence of insanity in immigrant groups appears to be a given, an unfortunate symptom of displacement and the impossibility of ever achieving a satisfying resolution to it. I believe it touches us all, but we cope differently. We do it in language.

AD: Yes. In all cultures. It happens with the turning away from the outside world and the unhealthy closing into oneself that leads to insanity. Perhaps, ethnicity is a good remedy to avoiding insanity. It might not be the right word, but, for me, it is a way of pointing to a place where these solitary people can meet somehow. Mainstream cultures now use equivocal terms such as *multiculturalism, crossculturalism*, and *transculturalism* to define an abstract territory where "strong" cultures can meet one another. That is not ethnicity. Ethnicity is really the creation of parallel systems, the process that rises from a weak position and which gradually leads to a different world view, whereby one finds correspondences (to use a Baudelarian term) that go beyond our own ethnic background, correspondences either to another group from the same ethnic background residing in a different territory or to another ethnic group from one or two separate territories.

PV: Ethnicity, as it has developed, describes well-defined, distinct, and separate entities but the description comes from outside. You find grouping and community within that, and you hold others at bay. Your definition of ethnicity is definitely the one that I subscribe to. It is about finding these parallel worlds. We do not have to have direct and continuous parallels, but we definitely need bridges that connect groups.

I am presently working in Little Italy here in San Diego, and looking at its history. Italians do not live in that area any more. Mexicans do. To say we cannot develop Little Italy to be Little Italy and reflect on the history of the Italians because Mexicans live there is stupid.

The present population of Mexicans and the past population of Italians share a history of displacement. There is a shared history with Spain, in its Colonial past at one level, but displacement is the number one common denominator. The Italians who lived in Little Italy were displaced from Italy. They came to San Diego, and they were again displaced by various elements of what we call "progress" into other areas. The people that live here now were displaced from Mexico for similar or different reasons, living in this area called "Little Italy." History is, after all, a shared experience. To look back at those commonalties, those causes and conflicts, is what should start the dialogue, not create a distance.

AD: Unfortunately, that vision is assuredly not the accepted vision, and it will never be, because such a world view would lead to the creation of parallel systems, which will never be recognized by mainstream culture or nationalist governments.

PV: Also, parallel systems deny territoriality, and they deny nationalism and they deny all those restrictive and exclusive systems.

AD: Exactly. That is why I have become very pessimistic about our destiny. For the next twenty-five years, we are going to be living in total obscurity, under the reign and terror of nationalism.

That means that, for the rest of my life as an adult, I will be no different than a beggar. It is a terrifying prospect.

When we break language, for example, we are trying to invent something new. Whatever it is that has to be invented is still in the process of being invented. The inventing is what's interesting. Because the invention is not seen, it is viewed as a threat, and it is this threat that mainstream culture fears. Regardless of one's ideological position, ethnic culture is today as essential as national mainstream culture used to be in the past. Ethnicity is irreversibly supplanting the mainstream's position in culture. Yet ethnic literature continues to be perceived as bad writing, ethnic film as bad filmmaking.

PV: Again its values are often overlooked by many within our own communities.

AD: That is because they want to talk about ethnicity and immigration in the past tense. And if you talk about ethnicity in the past tense, it is immediately viewed as harmless. It becomes harmful only if you analyze it in its proper context, as a never-ending process. As soon as you analyze it properly, then nationalist critics quickly retort, "You cannot talk about this issue because it is not Canadian, it is not Quebecois, it is not American, it is not Italian."

PV: Italy itself has never talked about its emigrant population. If Italy is talking about its immigrant population these days, it still seems to have done its best to discount, to forget, to dismiss its own history of emigration. Why did emigration start? We're going through the same thing that was happening during fascism. Back then we were saying that colonialism was necessary to provide land for the Italian population to thrive on. That is the greatest possible excuse for colonialism. It was, "Okay, don't emigrate, but emigrate." Do not emigrate to America . . . emigrate to Africa, because that is Italy. It was bull shit. You were still sending people away. Why do you not want them at home? The myth of too many people and not enough land and all that is bull shit too.

Those problems are emerging again today, with the Lega Nord wanting to separate. Italians fall back on those very same principles and stereotypes and myths.

Culture and linguistic legacy

AD: Going back to Quebec, I love Quebec in many ways. I learned a lot of stuff in Quebec. Where I do not agree with the separatists is that they are trying to turn an ethnic issue into a territorial one. What is interesting about Quebec is the fact that they are able to push the French culture from France to alter its course. Not only the Quebecois, so are the Haitians, the Black Africans who speak French, Arab Africans who speak French, the Arab world that speaks French, the Lebanese. The Belgians, for instance, who are but a handful of people can change a cultural issue touching on the destiny of the French peoples like never before. The same is true of the ex-French colonies in Asia. There are so many places where people speak French and each one of these peoples are forcing France to admit that France no longer is the sole proprietor of French culture. They yell non-stop: "France, you must open up." This is how the French-speaking peoples of the world created a commonwealth they name La Francophonie.

La Francophonie is a beautiful complex invention which I think goes beyond the notion of what once was the English Commonwealth. The Francophonie is a two-way street. The English Commonwealth was and remains a one-way street.

Because the anglophones form the second largest language group in the world with 456 million English-speaking people, there is an arrogance about them that baffles me. Compared to the Mandarin who form the largest language group in the world with 907 million people, the English seem forceful still about their cultural achievements. Perhaps they now feel a desire to change, perhaps this is why suddenly in America there is this weird blind-love for things anglo.

Hopefully this growing anglophilia is but the expression of a hidden desire to create something similar to the Francophonie which enables French culture to thrive. Maybe soon the Brits will no longer feel the urge to invest in the idea of a Commonwealth and will begin instead to nourish the idea of an "English-speaking community." Maybe that is why America has opened its doors to contemporary British films.

Why do we have this pressing reanalysis of British culture at a time when nationalism is dying? Perhaps there is a tacit urgency to unite the English-speaking people of the world. But how will they achieve this unification when one knows quite well that it is not necessarily true that all English-speaking people share a common culture?

I believe that the British were, in spite of themselves, less assimiliationists than the French? Unlike the French, the ultimate goal for the unification of English-speaking peoples can never be the creation of an English-speaking community. Coalition will have to be based on some other factor.

Yet this idea of a single community is exactly what the French strive for. There are now 126 million French-speaking people in the world. If France were to pull the plug it would lose the power it has attained thanks to the group strategy created by uniting all the French-speaking countries in the world.

The Portuguese-speaking peoples of the world have begun a similar network of countries. United they now form the eighth largest language group in the world with 189 million Portuguese-speaking people. They emulated their French counterpart and by establishing non-territorial links across the globe they have come out of the experience cultural winners.

The Spanish, the fourth largest group with 383 million Spanish-speaking people, will surely follow suit. The Germans, with 123 million German-speaking people, have begun the process for linguistic unification; one of the positive aspects behind the fall of the Berlin Wall was precisely this idea of uniting German-speaking people.

Italy is doing nothing in this regards. And what is happening to the Italians? They're not doing anything to help their situation. Statistics show that only 63 million people in the world speak Italian.

PV: In the introduction to *La letteratura dell'emigrazione* published by the Agnelli Foundation and edited by Marchand, the editor mentions this concept of Italofonia. But the problem there is that if you read the essays in the book, if you read his introduction, you realize that, in the Italian instance, it becomes an exclusive system. It is not an inclusive system. Italofonia is based on this false notion of Italian as a standardized language being presented as "the only way to properly speak Italian is this Italian."

This view deems all the Italians outside of Italy, all those masses of Italians outside of Italy who speak dialect, or who speak English, or French, or German as not part of that movement. So the book only includes writers who write in Italian, and nothing else. Which raises that issue which we love talking about: the *Italianisti,* who are the real problem. The relationship of the *Italianisti* to the Italian population in North America is problematic. But these *Italianisti* exist everywhere.

I am an *Italianista* myself. However, as far as studying Italian literature, there is a problem. That is what I run into all the time, this continuous need among *Italianisti* to define themselves as "real Italians." Their reasoning is based on language. What they perceive to be right or wrong about the way one expresses himself.

This illusion of being real Italians is achieved by denying their own emigration and immigration. Even though they have been here forty-five years, they do not regard themselves as emigrants or ethnics. Most of them have American citizenship or Canadian citizenship. It is just pure denial of emigration and displacement, mostly based on the notion that the people whom one calls emigrants are uncultured and are not to be dealt with. They are useless, they do not represent anything. It is very reactionary. It is a very reactionary view of a population.

Most of these people, I guess, would call themselves "progressive" or "leftist," whatever. I am sure they do not see themselves as reactionary or traditionalists or conservative in the negative term of conservative. They fall into the trap of considering the people who came to these countries for different reasons as being inferior. Because poor emigrants did not come here as professionals — to teach in universities or to run industry or companies, because they came here as workers, they are considered as not having a culture. They cannot, therefore, represent Italy. They are not Italians.

AD. The *Italianisti* define themselves against, *contro,* the other people that are here, right? But the paradox is that they themselves are not even considered by the Italians in Italy to be anything. So they are the real ghetto.

PV: They are definitely the real ghetto, but they have somehow managed to envision the walls they have erected around themselves as encircling those on the other side.

AD: They write books in a language that does not have an official status. They are unable to penetrate the official mainstream cultures on both side of the Atlantic: Not in America and not in Italy.

PV: What is the use of publishing books in Italian in North America if you have alienated the Italian community here. You are not speaking to them. Your initial assessment and your initial intention is to distinguish yourself from them, which you do at every level. So you are not writing in Italian for them. You are writing in Italian for the Italian audience. That Italian audience does not receive the books published in Italian, neither here nor there.

AD: How would they receive them, if they were to receive them?

PV: Some of these people are connected to certain writing communities in Italy, and they are able to introduce their writing there. They are successful to some degree. But they are not regarded as full fledged Italian writers. Italy is concerned with its own writers, the people who reside in Italy. For example, Calvino was always upheld as a great Italian writer, but there was always a question that came up in his regard: "Is he really an Italian writer?" He lived outside of Italy for such a long time. Can we call him an Italian writer because he writes in Italian? Is that the only criteria? Calvino is really a French writer. He is indicative of a certain condition. He was very much aware of his condition of displacement, and he illustrates that beautifully.

AD: The older I get the more I trust my feeling that Italian culture is based on displacement. Most writings by Italian writers are based on being exiled. From Ovid all the way to Calvino. How do you fit English language in this, or French language, or German language writing, in the Italic realities?

PV: I have talked about this before, and I am sure I have written about this issue. It does not matter what language you write in. You write in English, or you write in French and German and Italian. Whatever language you write in, it is like a dialect. It is yet another system that you juxtapose to the other systems that you have.

Most of us have some sort of dialect in our cultural background. We have learned Italian. We have learned English. We have learned French. Whatever language we have learned is just another part of what we are. Culture is a matter of subtraction and offering. It is loss along with gain. You lose something as you gain something. You put it together with what you have, and that's what you have to offer. And you offer it. It's not anal retentive, holding in at all costs . . .

I must remember to pronounce these words properly, or else I will be thought of as Italian or whatever. It is taking the mistakes and making something of those mistakes, and noticing how those mistakes emerge, and how they fold into what you have, and what will be.

Cultural suicide and cultural generation

AD: How about those writers who live here and who are no longer interested in the Italic culture? They might use elements from the Italic culture, but it is no longer their main interest. Their interest is to become part of a melting pot, part of the culture that reigns in Quebec, Canada, and the U.S.A. What is your view of these writers? Why does such a phenomenon take place?

PV: First of all, they are deceiving themselves, and they are attempting to deceive others. They are attempting to say that they are not interested, even if they are using ethnic subjects and themes. If they are not being sincere about ethnicity, then they are doing everyone a disservice. They come out of ethnicity, and obviously they have ties to it. So what is their intention in using these subjects?

One such writer can take a bunch of words and Italian concepts, and try a sort of misplaced satirist reading of them. Some of the shallowness of his relationship to Italian culture comes through, as does the influence of official cultures on how ethnics think of themselves and their cultures. That sort of venting strengthens stereotypes. Yet stereotypes are based on truth. To belittle what some people actually do is not a very intelligent thing to do. You must comment on culture differently. You do not take the argument of the official culture and turn it against the group from which you have emerged. It is just playing right into the hands of everyone who uses stereotypes of Italians in a derogatory way.

AD: Are they shedding elements of one culture in order to walk into a second culture naked — as a process for initiation?

PV: They are not going to go very far. If they stop writing about that stuff, they are not going to go very far. The reason such writers make it to the extent that they make it is because they wear certain items of clothing that define them. No matter how much they want to deny that investment and assimilate, they will always be defined as Italian

Canadians or Italians. Because if they were to write in a different manner, they would not get to where they are.

AD: You do not think so?

PV: They are still trapped with other Italians. They play a certain game that will lock them even more into having to use those elements. The more they deny those elements the more they get stuck with them. This is what is expected of them. They are doing what multiculturalism wants from "its" ethnic writers. In the process of doing what they are doing, they are also representing the death of their culture.

The representation of the culture is the undoing of the culture, though it will reemerge later on. The themes come back. As long as these writers continue representing the death of their culture, the undoing of their culture, the decimation of culture, especially in the representation of women, who are the generators of the body of diversity, the more they are expected to dish out this death of culture. In the end the members of the official culture will ask them to show that they are willing to be collaborators, to put it in terms of war: "Are you willing to be a collaborator and point a finger at your own kind?"

AD: You are aware that you are using strong terms.

PV: Oh yes, of course . . . they are very strong, Remember Wertmuller's *Seven Beauties?* What Pasqualino will do for survival in the concentration camp? He does not want to die, but at the same time he does not want to choose seven people who should be killed. If he does not choose seven people, he will be killed himself. So what is the choice? It is not an easy choice to make, but for some it is also a very easy choice.

AD. How do you see the future of young writers? As a publisher and editor, I am having a lot of problems with young Italian Canadians and Italian Americans, not necessarily young of age. Just young writers coming into the domain of literature. I have some difficulty with them, because I feel that they are not advancing in the same way as we did. How do they fit in, let us say, in a post-Verdicchio or in a post-Mary Melfi era? How they fit into that type of reality?

PV: I do not know if they have any interest in fitting into a post-Di Cicco, a post-Verdicchio or a post-Melfi period. Most will probably tell you that they do not really care about what we talk about as a history.

AD: But if you believe in tradition, this type of reasoning is invalid. Tradition is an important notion when it comes to writing. To want to imitate other writers that came before us is a natural process. Who do you think they will imitate, I mean, besides imitating other people from other cultures?

PV: I think they will imitate the writers who have been successful in the estimation of the mainstream. They will imitate sold-out ethnic writers who have made it. Young writers that are drawing close to me and have found my work useful are not imitating but interpreting me. Some of these young writers are of Italian background, but they are mostly non Italian: Chinese and Chicano. Possibly individuals whose sense of history of displacement is less dormant.

AD: That emulation coming from other peoples is a novel process, because we were until recently still in the laboratory, like you were saying. If the laboratory is there, then our findings on being and identity will be studied by those people who come after us in the historical context, in the emigration process. What happens to those of second, third, fourth generations, who will look at Gay Talese, who will look at John Fante, who will look at Pascal D'Angelo, Richard Gambino,

Anthony Valerio, Robert Viscusi? How do you think they will fit? Is there a future there, or is there death, or do you think that it does not have any future?

New writers, in my opinion, will emulate disappearing ethnics. I tell young aspiring writers, "Oh, my God, Italians have been writing for a hundred years why turn into a sold-out ethnic?" One makes it every time one sells out, but that doesn't mean that mainstream culture is going to accept you. If they do, it's a temporary contract which will soon come to an end. I tell writers not to expect me to turn them into sold-out ethnics, because I do not care to do so, nor do I have the political power to get them accepted by mainstream culture. I always tell aspiring writers who wish to become famous that I am not the right publisher for them.

On the other hand, when I see young writers like Fiorella De Luca Calce, Concetta Principe or Gianna Patriarca who all come from different historical backgrounds — one is from Naples, the second one is half Irish, half Italian, the third from near Rome and married to a New Zealander — when I look at their writing, I sigh in relief: "Now, this is more interesting." I feel these writers have done their homework. They are not necessarily saying, "I like what they did before me." I just feel that they have read us, and decided, "I think there's a flaming torch at the end of this tunnel which I want to carry."

When people say, "I want to be like so and so who has sold out" it is condemning. There are not many people that tell me they want to be like Marco Micone. I have never heard that: though he has given up the Italian cause and embraced the Quebecois separatists, I feel he is quite a writer. It is as though assimilating into Quebecois Canadianism, if I may express myself this way, were not enough. No, most writers want to be like the anglo sold-out ethnic writers whom I usually find lifeless, passionless, boring in the sense that one never feels like one wants to continue what a certain writer started. There is no need to continue where sold-out ethnic writers left off. It is as if they exhausted, and not always in the best of way, what there was to exhaust. Variations on these themes can be seriously boring and annoying.

PV: Young writers may be drawn to sold-out ethnics, firstly, because they are very successful and, secondly, because they give others a sense of freedom. But this is a false freedom since they designate their culture as a burden, and so present the possibility of shedding it in order to attain a newfound freedom. That is an illusion, as I have said so many times that I am getting bored by the issue.

It is the illusion that you can just shed who you are, take the clothes of culture off and walk naked into acceptance and assimilation. As if somebody is going to hand you a different set of clothes, clothes that are going to represent a different version of history and of who you are. You end up wearing what others want you to wear, without even getting to accessorize on your own. That is the problem.

It is an illusion that you can shed history. You cannot just narrate its end, the end of history. You might pretend that it is the end, but history always stays there. It stays here waiting for you to come along and get involved in it once more.

That concept of "the end of history" emerged at around the same time as certain books by sold-out ethnics were published and achieved fame. The idea that you can just turn off the tap on the influence of history and step out nice and clean is unreal. That you can be without responsibilities, without duties, with only rights and rewards is a lie.

Not simply because you should not do it, but because I do not think you have a choice in the matter. You will always be faced with history. Wherever you turn, you will be faced with history. At some point, someone will turn towards you, and impose a history on you. And then, if you have shed your clothes, and you have nothing to retort with, to answer back with, you will be lost.

Many young writers use sold-out ethnic writers as their only point of reference, because they see history as a burden. They interpret its diminishment as a victory. They are in for a big disappointment along the way somewhere.

AD: Is it paradoxical that some speak about Italian culture only as a post-fascist phenomenon? What do you think about people skipping fascism, that dark period of history in Italy but also in Canada, which Filippo Salvatore and Roberto Perin analyze, and to some extent, even Antonino Mazza in his preface of his translation of Mario Duliani's novel, *City Without Women*. It is unfortunate that Nino Ricci avoids fascism in *Lives of the Saints,* as though he did not want to deal with the delicate theme. I could not but mention it. *Fabrizio's Passion* starts with the war.

PV: We have to mention fascism. It is, again, that history that cannot be denied. If you turn your back to fascism, it will bite you in the ass.

AD: We have to talk about the burning bodies and the smell of burnt flesh. I think it is unavoidable that we talk about those horrors. Italians did not have a Nuremberg trial. Yet I think it has to be done somehow.

PV: Even though Italian culture in the post-war period is mostly left leaning or influenced, the institutions of fascism are still very much present. Pasolini talked about them, and his talking about these issues led to his assassination. A number of people talk about it. We have Andreotti as a remnant of it. We have Craxi as an example of it. We have Bossi *duro* and truly part of it. We have all sorts of people as living examples of fascism. We have political parties in Italy that are an example of fascism. Fascism is not over. You cannot say it is post-fascism in the sense that it does not exist anymore, or that it is done and gone. You have to deal with fascism in the present tense. People do not want to talk about fascism the same way that they do not want to talk about the Mafia. These are realities. They are still very much with us.

We talked about film making. The Italian film makers of the 1970s went back to make films that were based in fascist times, during the war, to warn people of what was still going on and what the potential for a relapse was. What a beautiful film Ettore Scola's *A Special Day* was! Not only its photography, not only as a film, but as a document. The message was loud and clear: "Watch out! Fascism is alive! In different ways, but it is happening. Don't forget!"

AD: We are the children of the 1950s. We lived the sequels of fascism. Our parents experienced it firsthand, they went to school under fascism. I am intrigued by how fascism snuck into families without our being aware of it. And I find it incredible that the *Italianisti* in America do not really analyze it. Few of these *Italianisti* write or talk about fascism.

PV. To talk about the history of fascism and the legacy of fascism is to admit that you are somehow working within the system that fascism set up. Because we are still working within that system to some extent. Many of the institutions in Italy are fascist. The idea of *Italianità,* for example, that has become so dear to Italian American and Italian Canadian writers and critics, no matter how you argue around it, as a unifying concept of Italian identity, is proto-fascist. For some people to stress that one does not speak proper Italian unless one comes from Florence, and the only proper Italian is this language and not dialects is very fascistic in spirit.

We participate in this sort of fascist attitude every day. That is why we do not want to talk about fascism. We would have to start delineating and describing the mechanisms of fascism, and soon we would be saying: "Whoops, am I guilty of this too?" This is why fascism is not addressed. It is best to talk about post-fascism, as if fascism was dead and gone.

AD: Today it is called nationalism. There is one writer whose name I will not mention who got insulted when I said that fascism and nationalism are one and the same thing.

PV: Because the person was probably a "real Italian."

AD: But he has been living in America for forty years! He might even has been born here!

PV: There is no "real Italian" anywhere in the world. There is no such thing, and particularly not in Italy. There are no real Italians, as the current sociopolitical situation there illustrates.

AD: Do you think that your writings, if they survive, will help the Italian culture? The Canadian culture? or the American culture? Where do they fit?

PV: That is a hard question. I just know my work receives more attention in the U.S.A than it does in Canada. That is all I can say now. I do not know if it will do anything. It is hard to say if it will advance anything or pull others down with it.

AD: That was one question that was asked of me many years ago. "Do you think that your writing will help Quebec culture?" I do not feel that we advance any one particular culture. We advance the culture that accepts us. It all depends on what mainstream cultures will say about our work.

PV: Isn't this linked to what you asked before: "Which young writers read me?" A certain culture accepts my writing, yet I can't say with assurance that "this is Italian writing, therefore, it has to advance Italian Canadian or Italian American writing." If people are not interested, our work is not going to advance anything. It comes down to which culture is interested in our writing.

AD: Do you think they are interested? I do believe that they are not interested. In one of my poems I ask, "Who are you writing for? The eighteen year-old girl or a forty year-old man?" I wrote in French because there was a potential readership, and people seemed to be interested in buying my stuff. In English, the silence is deadening. This is one reason why I do not collect my writings very much anymore, I do not feel anybody is interested. Not the Italians. Not the Italics. Yet Guernica is putting out these books that sell. But I do not know who buys them. It has always been a mystery to me: Which persons buy our books?

PV: I am always surprised, too, when I go somewhere and people have my books, or if they know my books. Obviously, I am glad. But it surprises me that my books have traveled that distance.

AD: Of course, books travel. They may not travel very far, but they do travel.

The Association of Italian Canadian Writers

PV: The first meeting of the Association of Italian Canadian Writers took place in Vancouver in 1986. It was decided that there should be a meeting after Italy. So, in 1986, we met in Vancouver. And, as far as I am concerned, that was the best one. Why? Because we still had that freshness. We did not hate each other yet. We were still trying to discover what the hell we were all about. It was still an ego trip for us all. It was party time.

AD: In 1988, it immediately became political in Toronto. Correct?

PV: Actually, do you know when it became political? Almost right away in 1986, when we created the Berzani prize. As soon as the prize was established, it became political. It was in Vancouver that we decided that we should formalize the group and turn it into a real association. Dino Minni, Joseph Pivato, yourself and me. A number of writers were there.

AD: Remember, at the restaurant, it was . . .

PV: On Commercial Drive, I think. Anyway. Then we established the prize with the Italian Community Center there. The first one went to an Italian Canadian. Somehow, the Berzani prize just . . .

AD: Disintegrated.

PV: It became a prize of the community center. They sort of took it over. It became a political vehicle for the people involved more directly in the administration of the prize. Gradually they lost interest in maintaining any tie with Italian Canadians writers.

AD: Is the prize still around?

PV: It is still around. But it became a general multiculturalism prize; it moved away from its initial idea of promoting Italian Canadian literature. It became a way for interested people to say: "Look, we're giving prizes to other communities." It was a way to garner support from other communities, a very political move.

AD: I no longer participate. Guernica never sends books there.

PV: It does not matter. You would not get it anyway!

AD: That is so funny! The ironies! That is the image of our community. We create things, then we open them up, and we are no longer eligible by our own criteria.

PV: We are our own worst enemies. But I really think, in that case, it was a setup. There again a legacy of fascism, clientelism. Dino Minni passed away. I had recently moved to Los Angeles. For example, Perticarini was completely excluded. The only people who were involved in that prize had no interest in the Association but saw the prize as a vehicle for self-promotion.

AD: In 1987 or '88, something happened. I forget what it was. I did not want to go. I thought that there would be . . . I knew there would be a lot of in-fighting.

PV: You did not come to the York conference?

AD: No. I boycotted it. Something was going on. I knew that Marco Micone and Filippo Salvatore were going to go at each other on the question of Quebec separation.

PV: There was some of that in York. Our first meeting in Toronto . . . we were trying to meet in Toronto because it is the center of Canada, and we ended up in York and we hardly even went into Toronto. We went for one reading in Toronto, that was it. We were out at York University because it has the Elia Chair. Joseph Pivato was there as the Elia chairperson at that time.

AD: Pivato organized that conference.

PV: It was sort of an isolating experience, because we were on this campus, and never actually connected with the world. None of the writing community from Toronto came.

AD: Why should they?

PV: Well, exactly. We were trying to get recognition from the more general community, to generate interest in our work.

AD: The Ottawa conference organized by Francesco Loriggio was interesting. However, I felt that you were right to point out how the readings were unfairly divided.

PV: My criticism was not directed at the organizer but at the Association as an institution. The divided readings had already begun at York.

AD: It was awful to separate venues between those who were considered important and those who were less important. It probably was not done consciously, but only a handful of men and women ever stayed for the afternoon readings.

PV: The evening reading downtown is the one where we created our own elite, by pushing the same group of writers. At York already, we had a downtown reading. The ones who read there were the usual ones, mostly Torontonians perceived as the stars of Italian Canadian writing. They read with the locals; while all the other writers (the non-locals) read at York. It is kind of useless to set up readings like that; readings should provide exposure for those who are flown in from out of town. We have been guilty of that mistake all along. Except in Montreal, there we read all together, didn't we?

AD: Of course.

PV: Five minutes each.

AD: Three minutes each. We had the whole evening. That theater was given to us for free. We only had to pay $15 for the cleaning maintenance. That was thanks to Dimitri Roussopoulos from

Black Rose Press, who had the connection there. I decided, this is going to be the Ed Sullivan Show for Italian Canadian writers. I really wanted to make everybody feel important. This reading was going to be a show. And it turned out fairly well. Joseph Maviglia came with his guitar, and he did his stuff. He wanted to have half an hour to perform, but I said, "No. What you're going to do is to appear in between sections. There were twenty-one writers in all. We had three sections of seven writers, he played three times. He did the music. It became relaxing. People walked out, walked in, whatever happened happened. I thought it was okay.

PV: I think it worked.

AD: But I was reproached then, in 1992, at the Winnipeg conference for having treated all the writers equally. All the "star writers" were disappointed that they were given the same amount of time as the non-stars. They forget that even major acts such as The Beatles and The Rolling Stones could only sing one or two songs on the Ed Sullivan Show! They had the same air time as any other performer. Yet they still made it big. That was the wager. They had to make their impact on the audience in a fixed time limit. The trick is not to blab on for two hours, presenting the premises of the work to be read, but to read the work and let the audience be judge. If you're good, you're good. And, in Montreal, everyone was great.

PV: The Association began to fragment in Winnipeg mostly because some writers thought we should only be talking about writing. Some of the writers thought they should be reading at least half an hour each. But we are not only writers. There are artists, academics, some of us are a bunch of those things together. You did well with the Montreal readings, by putting them in three-minute slots, by not giving anybody the upper hand. When these meetings take place, organizers should take it onto themselves to book readings in the downtown area of the city where the conference is scheduled, and to organize one reading alone on one of the evenings.

AD: Do you think the Association should survive? Do you think it will survive?

PV: I am not sure if it should survive. I, myself, feel very ambivalent. Winnipeg has had an effect even on the Association's modest newsletter. I recently proposed a number of new directions in our policy that I thought might be useful for the Association. If we are going to exist as a real association rather than just a club that meets every two years to praise ourselves or argue, then we really have to look at what sort of function and activism we wish for ourselves as a group. As president of the Association, I proposed four plans that I would like to see us do.

First, we should begin a Canon Project, something to push our books in bookstores. Every month propose a book, send the suggestion out to the membership, who would then buy the book and ask others to buy it. So and so has published this book, everyone go out and buy it. Go to your bookstores and order it. If they don't have it, ask the bookstores to order it. I have participated in the one here in the U.S.A. That is how I came to boycott some bookstores. They would not order the books, because they said they did not deal with that distributor. Soon it became a political problem. So I said, "Well, if you don't want to order the books that I need for my classes, books that I'm interested in, then I will not buy anything at all from you until you change your policy." We should be doing the same up in Canada.

Second, I also proposed that the group look into the media and follow up on how it portrays Italians, Italian Americans, and Italian Canadians in the news. A small committee should be formed in order to collect articles and maybe respond to some of the issues raised by the press.

Third, we must establish links with communities in every city. We really need, for example, a women's caucus within the association which would deal with women's issues.

I got only one letter from a young woman writer saying that these were good ideas. But that was all. I do not know why. If we propose a community workshop, it should not be for us, so we could sit around and talk about our own writing, but for the members of the community.

Finally, we need to begin to collect more of the histories of the communities, the personal histories, a workshop on collecting personal histories, and to create archives.

Preserving culture

AD: Archives are what will be passed on from one generation to the other. There is a new generation of men and women who want to study available archives, who wish to have access to important documents of our past and present.

PV: Imagine if somebody had interviewed our grandparents, or if somebody went in to interview my parents, for example, or your parents.

These are the people who do not have the time or inclination to write, or are unable to write the stories that form our cultural background. I say, Get their story! I am trying to follow my family history now, and there are memory blocks. I reach a certain point in events and things disappear. Imagine if people had interviewed some of the first generation immigrants in Canada, what would be available!

AD: Should we blame the educated upper classes for having discouraged the lower class to analyze their own history? Take, for example, literary archives. I have in my possession the birth of all the books that Guernica has published. No matter what book I do, there is a history to it. And that history is fundamental to the understanding of what happens. That is what makes literary history indispensable. Yet that aspect of my editorial work is going to be destroyed, if no one buys Guernica's archives. I am going to have to destroy them, because I have too many boxes stored. They are taking over my house, my parents' house, and my sister's house. Literally. At one point I am going to have to do something. I find it incredible that no institution that I have approached has shown any interest.

PV: You can begin to donate parts of your archives, and sell others. For example, University of California in San Diego has an archive, and they buy archives that are related to the ones that they have, obviously. It is a matter of starting to feed the material. You have Nicole Brossard's stuff and they have Brossard papers here. You also have some Daphne Marlatt papers related to her book, *Two Women in a Birth*. You have my papers. You have people who are connected to people in the U.C.S.D. archive in so many ways. Jerome Rothenberg is in those archives. The people found in these archive are all interconnected somehow. Daphne Marlatt and Nicole Brossard communicated with Bett Miller here. Quickly this is how files begin to branch out.

You should donate a small chunk of your archives that includes some of these South Californian connections, and tell U.C.S.D., "I've got boxes and boxes, if you're interested." The unfortunate thing is that these archives are outside of Canada and your archives should remain in Canada.

AD: They should, but no one in Canada cares about Guernica's archives.

PV: Maybe it does not really matter if your archives are in Canada or not.

AD: Canadians criticize us for being ethnic. When we rap on their doors and offer our services, they usually turn us down. What do you want me to do? I am aware that we are offering new Canadian visions. Why should critics and writers systematically disregard our world class books? When people ask me, "Why do you take such a radical position on such and such an issue?" I reply: "I was pushed in to this position. I never wanted it to be this way. I was born in Canada. Why do you push me into this isolation? Do you think I'm going to commit suicide? I'm not going to commit suicide. I'm going to learn to adjust myself, find ways to make do." But in the meanwhile I am stuck with these archives which I really think is a sin, a capital sin. No, not capitalism, but a capital sin.

I keep everything because I gather information. I am a collector. One day out of the blue a competitor publisher phoned me up before I left Montreal. He advised me, "Tony, keep everything. You've got a great archive. Don't throw anything away." And I said, "Why are you interested?" He said, "I know what you're going through, and I'm sure you want to throw everything away. Don't. That stuff that you have is very valuable."

I was surprised that there would be a fellow writer and publisher who would care enough for me and phone me up one day out of the blue to tell me not to take a fit against my archives. No one in the Italian Canadian community cares. Even though these archives could entail tax write-offs. One would expect some rich Italian foundation to be interested by this stuff and denote our files to some university with a large population of Italian students.

PV: Exactly. They should be interested in beginning an archive. It seems it would benefit them tremendously.

AD: But archives are a highly politicized matter. We are right back where we started: the professors in power, the *Italianisti,* are simply not doing their job. The old guard constantly pushes the newcomers away. The attitude is so typically Italian, really. In a community as rich as ours, the wealthy and powerful, instead of helping one another and being proud of what artists produce, do not care one bit about what writers have accomplished on the artistic front.

PV: Yes. We try to get in each other's way. Everyone's out for himself.

AD: That is the problem with the Association. We are a bunch of egoists who are doing nothing for the well-being of the many. There is no serious desire to attain higher levels of well-being. The Association is still around thanks to a couple of people, who have been working their heads off to keep it alive, and paradoxically, these are the most radical minds of the group, the ones who in fact do not need the Association to keep doing their work.

PV: There seems to be no interest whatsoever in continuing it, there is no involvement. Take the absence of response to my proposals as an indication of the interest. There is no interest. And you can count on those who complain the most to be the least active.

AD: Some writers expect the Association to help them become famous. They get upset when they realize that the Association cannot help them become famous, since an association serves the interests of the group and not those of the individual. Some writers complain, "Look! All of the famous Italian Canadian writers are not here."

Who can these famous writers be? I ask myself. Is something wrong with an Association of writers who are not famous? I don't think so. This is the same sort of comments that the governmental funding institutions give me. "All the

famous Italian writers are not with Guernica."
Big deal, I say.

The "famous" writers they are alluding to
have been or will eventually be with Guernica at
some point in their career. Guernica is the place
they will turn to when there will be no other place
to turn to. The real issue being raised is: "Are the
many writers that Guernica publishes less valuable than those who do not publish with Guernica?"

What does being famous mean if we do not
respect a writer's work? I tried working with "famous" writers, it got me nowhere. I simply cannot
work with a writer who uses a publisher like pe-
troleum jelly. There must be mutual respect between writer and publisher, otherwise what is the
use of working together? A publisher is not a
means to an end.

Some writers attack the Association for not
lobbying their fame and so get really bitter. They
blame the rest of us for their misfortune. But what
these writers do not understand is what the star
system is about and so fail to appreciate the *raison
d'être* for an Association of Italian Canadian writers. They do not fully grasp what working in culture is all about. Writers who were fortunate
enough to get published at one point in their ca-

reer, now realize that publishing means nothing. Today it has become almost impossible to reach your audience. Most of the time people have never heard of you, despite the fact that you may have published extensively. Many writers do not want to admit that there are more serious issues at stake than becoming famous. Writers do not even openly acknowledge that they need a group to get their works accepted, to protect their copyright, to make sure grants are made available to all equally, and to receive a fair representation on boards and in institutions that handle millions of dollars dedicated to culture, money which most of the time never makes its way down to ethnic writers and associations.

Other writers feel that to associate themselves to a group of ethnic writers would undermine their chances of becoming famous. They do not want to be seen in the company of scum — whether it is because they have not come out of the ethnic closet, or they feel they do not need to come out, or perhaps they are just too scared to come out, fearing there will be reprisals, or that they will be ostracized by the star system invented by mainstream culture. The truth of the matter is that they are probably right. They *would* be ostracized if they were to associate with scum like us.

Mainstream culture has its ways of keeping ethnics from uniting together.

And so the unslaught of negativity begins: "Why go with Guernica? Guernica is only a small press that never publishes Canadians. When will Guernica start publishing Canadians?" As if Canadians with different sounding names could not be Canadians. Many still expect Canadians to look like the talking heads seen in those supper time news reports on TV.

PV: Many attack the Association, suggesting that it undermines one's success. If the Association doesn't continue, what do you think might happen or should happen? Do you think there should be a smaller association, a smaller group in order to carry on certain functions and establish contact with the extended community? Are these not the functions of an association like ours?

AD: We should look at other writer's associations in different parts of the continent, say in Quebec, Union des écrivains québécois, for solutions to our problems. The only way any association will thrive is if it becomes indispensable. Right now, as it is, our association *is* dispensable. We would have to transform our inutility into efficacy. If the Association would, let's say, win a copyright infringement case, then it would be seen as valuable. Recently, Marisa De Franceschi went through a copyright infringement case. This should have been an association case, since the infringement affected us all, not just Guernica and De Franceschi. There are a hundred people in the Association, had all of the membership signed a petition the case would have attracted some attention from the press. Press coverage is all we could have expected since we simply don't have the power to win even an outright copyright infringement: And who would pay the bill? Is copyright for the rich alone? Imagine: as individuals we neither have the money nor the political clout to win a justified case in court. An association could help here.

The Association is a club. Because it is a club, it is not going to go anywhere. In order to boast our membership my goal was always to invite every kind of artist to join the Association: journalists, professors, critics, and why not painters, photographers, musicians. Maybe we should call this larger umbrella group The Italian Community Artists' Association. This way we would have enough resources to offer specialized services. Membership requirement could be none other than the desire for an artist to help one's ethnic group for the good of the larger community.

PV: One no longer is simply an Italian Canadian. One is a writer. Yet there is a portion of people who use identity as a convenience, as a vehicle to get a grant or to publish a book. They then turn up their nose to anyone who tries to make identity a viable subject for both cultural and political action. One makes a decision that, if nothing else, is political. Which is that identity must be denied and degraded because that is what the host culture requires of its initiates.

The stage that is so despised is one that every new culture must go through. We have certain themes and subjects to talk about, mostly nostalgic ones. That stage must be recognized and addressed. Unfortunately, and this places the blame on the other side now, the nostalgic mode tends to take over both the writers and the critics. That is what institutionalized multiculturalism requires of so-called ethnic or minority groups. At that level I understand the frustration of those who want to distance themselves from ethnicity.

Attacks on Guernica and the Association are stuck in that rut, and there's no way of coming out. In the end it is one's own writing that one must deny.

If the investigation of identity and social position is only a stage, with no effective influence on "real" writing, then it also means that one must write as an identityless individual. That may be possible, but I cannot imagine it.

AD: The more you think that you are dealing with nostalgia, the more you realize that it is not so. If nostalgia is analyzed properly, nostalgia leads to political questions: "Why is it that they built a highway over my Little Italy?" or, "Why is it that my Little Italy was destroyed." Nostalgia at its best must be political and not personal.

PV: Nostalgia can definitely be a way to politicization, a way to politicize your contemporary existence. In fact, I believe that multiculturalism at the grassroots level is nothing more than nostalgia that has led to activism. The Chicano movements and the Black movements are all based in some sort of nostalgia, but not the sort of nostalgia that bogs you down in the past.

AD: Here is an example of nostalgia showing its monstrous face to society. One year the Quebec writers' union asked for a list of possible honorary writers. So I nominated a bunch of English writers from Quebec. They were all turned down. I asked, "Why are you turning them down?" They answered: "They are English writers." I said, "So am I. And I'm in this union as an English writer. I'm talking to you in French, but I'm an English writer. I've been here since 1979. You didn't invite me as a Quebecois. I wrote in French earlier, in 1973, but that book you were unaware of. I came here as an English writer. Therefore, you're telling me that I am not worthy of this union?" I had to quit that union after this incident.

PV: That is what post-war Italy was all about. It was supposed to be a period of national re-building but of course we know that it developed otherwise. Or else, why would emigration continue to the extent that it did? My family came to Canada in the 1960s. What did the economic boom do for so many southerners? Vittorio De Sica was decrying the egoism that took over during that period. He saw it as a particularly strong problem. And he was right. Andreotti, Craxi, and Bossi represent that egoism and it certainly affects the structure, the politics, the social and economic aspects of a society.

AD: We come from post-war Italy, so we have been brainwashed one way or another by Mussolini. Most of us do not realize that. We all have Mussolini in our background. Whether our parents were against Mussolini or for him is secondary. We all went to Mussolini schools. When I went to the village, I asked where my parents went to school, and they said, "This is where they went." And I said, surprised: "Oh, at the one Mussolini built?" The same thing can be said about Canada and its influence on us.

What is the difference between the French Italian Canadian writers and English Italian Canadian writers? And how do others, like myself, who went through both systems cope? Those who went to the French system have been totally brainwashed. Those who went to the English system have been totally brainwashed. The third group, the ones that went to English schools in a French environment and those (of the future) who will go to a French school in an English environment, may not be as brainwashed, because they are able to see through both systems and distiguish the good from the bad.

Regrettably, this group of men and women, those who are or were forced to identify with both systems, may not be brainwashed but certainly are screwed up. They are different. Mary Melfi, Filippo Salvatore, Marco Micone and myself are different. There is something very different about the way we perceive Canada and America. We were able to receive intellectual nourishment from not only two cultures — the Italic and the French or English; we were forced to learn from a third reality: the Other official Canadian culture. This triangulation of cultures is very unique. We stand at a very strategic point in Canadian history. We fell in love at once with the French culture and the English culture and the Italian culture. We also had to despise each one of these cultures. A hatred which often left us cultureless.

To use a Freudian image: we had not only one father to hate, we had three fathers to discard. Normally Micone's separatist stance should represent exactly the position these culturally "triangular" writers should take, whereby Canada does not exist. However this has not been the case. Each one of us has chosen a distinct and subjective position in Canadian history. Our view of Canada is unique and almost subversive. It is neither French nor British, it is Other.

But a serious problem arises when you are a federalist like Salvatore and Melfi. One realizes that theirs is no different than Micone's position: paradoxically, their path to the future will never lead them towards Canada. At least, not the Canada we normally hear on the radio, read in the papers, or watch on TV.

I am a perfect example. Having left Montreal for Toronto, I am no longer considered a Quebecois, nor am I considered a "real" Canadian. I am in Canada as an emigrant, despite the fact that I am a Canadian born citizen. People keep on joking about this "emigrant" facet of my citizenship all the time.

Yet the Quebecois separatist position has become an unbearable solution for me. I used to be, and in many ways still am, a believer of a separatist Quebec. I believe that Quebec should separate. It is not that they are wrong for being separatists, nor is it wrong for some Quebecois to want to be part of Canada. What is wrong is the fact that living in Quebec people acquire a false notion of what it means to be a Canadian. There is no Canada in the Quebecois mind, and not necessarily because Canada is English. There can only ever be a Quebecois Canada, which happens to be French-speaking. Where does that leave us?

The goals to attain and strive for rarely cross over to Canada. When a child grows up in Quebec, he helps build a French Canada, a French Quebec, a Quebec Canada, never a Canada Canada. This is normalcy. He will not succeed otherwise. He is inspired to succeed with that view of Canadian culture. That culture becomes Quebecois through and through, and, paradoxically. if one chooses to become a part of that "regional" culture, one is incredibly drawn to a more open view of the world, to a world that will never exist in the mind of the English Canadian.

When people say that Quebec is cosmopolitan, it is to this complex phenomenon that they are referring to. The truth is that Quebec is a much more homogenous society than English Canada. It is English Canada that should rightly be called cosmopolitan and not French Quebec, where the proportion of ethnic communities is substantially smaller than the large ethnic groups in English Canada. So why is it then that English Canada has not come to terms with its essentially pluricultural being? Why has English Canada not come out of the ethnic closet yet?

PV: I think it is time to be giving back, to make the work valuable in a more general sense, rather than just go for ourselves. Maybe that is too idealistic. I am becoming more and more involved with the Italian community here in San Diego. At one of the first meetings I attended a man said to me, "Why did you come here — to ask for help? This happens all the time. We see university people come down into the community for something and then they disappear; we never see them again. We would like to see somebody who comes in because they want to join us."

People only go to the communities when they need money. In my case I had to remind him that I started doing the history of the community which led to a documentary film, and that I had not really asked for anything myself. All I asked for was material to include in the history project for their community. The problem, however, is that they do not see this project as a project working for them. They see it as something that will benefit me and not them.

The difference is that I am from a generation that is different from those other *Italianisti* generations, people who came over from Italy to start departments and to work at the universities.

I am part of a generation that ended up at the universities almost by accident. I told the man, "I'm from the same side as you are and we have to begin to open up the universities."

I have been working *with* the community. Not to go there and impose my voice as an academic or as a professor or as a writer, but as someone trying to take part in the community life. People in institutions are able to manage the social strata outside of the institution much more effectively than ever before. Some of us are still very reluctant to state outright, publicly, "Yes, I'm working class. I didn't come to this country as a professional. I grew up as an immigrant, in an immigrant community, a working-class community."

Once you have made it to the university, what is your function? I want to go back to Gramsci again, and speak about the role of the intellectual. It is our role, it is our duty and our responsibility to emphasize the presence of that social strata in the institution, and to set up lines of communication with the outside world.

Idealistic? Maybe? I am not giving up. I do not think we can change the system totally, but I am willing to give it my best to cause a mutation. I see myself as a mutagen working on the genetic material of the institution. My parents did not go to university. They did not finish high school, they did not finish elementary school. These facts put you in a different space. There are a lot of people who are reluctant to actually state that they are from such a background and to work out of that experience.

For many of us illiteracy is an immediate and familiar reality. It is not lost in generational distance. The jump we have made is incredible and it is important that it be acknowledged. I guess that is the danger of most immigrant and minority groups at the social level.

The children have leaped beyond the limits of the wildest imagination of the host culture. As such, they represent a threat to the survival of what is considered official or dominant culture. That threat is diminished, however, if people can be convinced that their own culture is backward and unimportant, that it is a prison to be denounced and escaped.

So we have the phenomenon: "Yes, I'm Italian, but I'm not like them, like the immigrants. I'm a real Italian." How many times have we heard: "My parents' culture, Italian culture, is oppressive."

AD: I stick too closely to a particular community of writers and intellectuals. Because the writers I publish come from one regional community or another, because I publish *from within* communities, our writers are considered lesser writers by those critics who think they, on the other hand, belong to *no* community, who believe they are national, therefore mainstream. There is no such thing as a national writer. This sort of appellation is an invention. Even the mainstream is now considered a regional community, a community no different from any other regional or ethnic community.

PV: Guernica writers do not represent what this country would like to present as its intellectuals. Do you expect Canada to be eager to be represented by the offspring of peasants and laborers? You've heard some say it: "I'm not a peasant, and my parents were not peasants. Why should I be interested in this stuff?"

AD: Most of our writings are about the lower class, whether you like it or not. They are about displacement. Such themes make some readers uncomfortable. They prefer solidity, rocks, immutable truths, that is lies. Ours is a vision that is not easily available in literature. Or if it is available, it is available as a degradation of something that was once good. Something else was once more important. Someone fell here and, by falling down, he is showing us this vision of the fall. William Burroughs and Charles Bukowski are a good examples of a literature of the "fall." Theirs is a vision of what to expect in hell. It is a modern visit in hell. "You too might end up here, but, this is temporary, I am just visiting. I can get out if I want to, and come back to real life."

This is a luxury that is available only to the fortunate. It is very rare that you get lower class people who make it through. I do not wish to imply that our literature is principally one of victimization, it isn't. Yet there is quite a difference between the "visitors" to hell and those who permanently live in hell.

PV: That's why I use *Devils in Paradise* as the title for my collection of essays. That is an important notion regarding our identity abroad and in our own land. French, German, and British travelers to Italy went there to experience hell, knowing that they would be able to leave at any time. When the people who lived there emigrated, they invaded another sort of paradise. The emigrant, the outsider as the devil, disturbing the waters of paradise. But we want to be angels! The Canadian mainstream is God.

AD: The press is not very kind to we poor devils. Once the press did speak about our devilish works, but that is no longer the case. From curiosity they have gone to total silencing, to the point of people telling me: "Do you still publish?" and magazines telling me, "We never got the books," even though I had twice sent the books to the magazines and sent people invitations to our launchings. They just don't want to be bothered about reviewing our kind of stuff. There is an editor from an ethnic studies magazine who said to me: "Well, your books don't fall under the label ethnicity." If the mainstream thinks our books are not mainstream, and the ethnic press does not think they are ethnic, what are they then?

PV: You have to fall into some category that someone else defined. Your work was getting reviews, though, when you were doing mostly Quebecois writers, no? In Quebec.

AD: That is not exactly true. I remember very well having to defend certain writers that I had published. I remember when I had to defend myself for having published gay poet André Roy, one of my favorite Quebec poets, in fact, a language poet whose texts no one considered gay. I keep on saying Quebec. I hate that. Because Quebec is part of Canada, so we should be talking about a Canadian poet and not a Quebecois poet. André Roy is a major voice in Canada. He was one of the first writers to talk about being gay not just as content but in its form as well. He is the first young writer who talked about being left-wing. He is also the first Canadian poet to talk about psychoanalysis. So Daniel Sloate and I decided to do his selected poems. As soon as the book came out, people started criticizing it. One of them wrote an article in *Books in Canada,* denouncing the fact that these books were actually being given grants to get published! André Roy had just won the Governor General's Award!

As you can see many people know nothing about what the other side of this country is doing. People are so blinded by their own region that they do not see the whole picture of the country. I feel we belong to the few Canadians who actually know what is being done on both sides of this bicultural inferno.

PV: What was Mr. Writer criticizing?

AD: Roy's obscenity. The lack of craft in the writing, how awful the poetry was.

PV: It's kind of ironic, years later, that Mr. Writer actually approached you to publish some of his books. I studied with Mr. Writer at the University of Victoria.

AD: We ran into him in Victoria. That type of behavior is what I constantly have to face for being involved in cultural production. The fact that we are being silenced does not mean that our work is no good. They are actually silencing a part of the culture in Canada, and basically, for me, that equals censorship. This sort of close-mindedness on the part of both official cultures propagates a false notion of what Canada is to the rest of the world.

PV: What does it mean when someone tells you that your writing does not fall into the dictates or the parameters of multiculturalism? It means that "You do not belong. You should probably leave Canada, because you don't write in the way that we think Canadians should write." It does not make sense to deny cultural development and identity.

AD: When was the last time you got reviewed?

PV: Uh, mmm. Let's change the subject.

AD: When was the last time you got reviewed? Honestly?

PV: The last time I got reviewed was probably a year or two years ago, and it was for a book of translations. The Giorgio Caproni book, I believe. I can count on . . . I do not even need both my hands . . . the number of reviews that I have had of my poetry.

Every time that someone has reviewed my books, he or she commented that "Pasquale Verdicchio doesn't know how to write English. Maybe he writes his poems in Italian, and translates them in English. He should have a native English speaker look at them." They did not even try to see if maybe I was doing something with the language.

AD: Funny . . . a reviewer criticized *Fabrizio's Passion* by raising that exact same point, using the same words. They said that I did not know how to write. It was really disgusting. I wrote back, asking the editor: "Well, what does it mean to know how to write?" No wonder the grant institutions in Canada keep cutting our grants; they think we are publishing shit.

PV: Oh, I read your letter to the Editor. Interestingly enough, that is exactly the same problem that "third world" immigrants in Italy have. When we meet so called "real Italians" here, they use the same argument against us. They totally dismiss the potential of alternative ways of expression. They require a standardized mode of expression, and it has to follow their rules. They cannot see how this linguistic audacity actually generates culture. Or, is it maybe that they need to kill this audacity? By ignoring and by questioning our literary abilities and qualifications, and by denouncing the work as being of questionable quality, they are killing culture.

AD: I am preoccupied by this attitude, as a publisher and also as a writer, because I must tell you . . . I am going through a literary crisis right now. Maybe, I should stop writing. This is one reason why I produced my music CD *Night Talks*.

PV: These attacks are indicative of the fact that we ourselves are falling victim to what it means to be ethnic. We have bought the formula. No matter how often some editors denounce the "nonna and pizza" type of writing, if you look at the poetry they publish that is what they expect from ethnic writers.

AD: That is the only sort of writing that has been taken seriously.

PV: It has become too easily absorbed and accepted. I would like to think that we have a wider range in culture. We complain about other people using stereotypes but what about us? Even when someone writes about Gilbert Sorrentino. Because he does not fit into the tight ethnic mold they are quick to declare that he has betrayed his background or has lost touch with it.

One of the questions I always get asked is "Do you write with an audience in mind?"

AD: Many writers say no. I am surprised by that statement, because personally I am starting to be more and more frightened by what I say and write. Obviously it means that, somewhere in my mind, I have the word police. I find it less and less possible for me, even though my readership is one person, to ignore what that person might think of my writing. I am scared. I am really, really scared.

I came to La Jolla to write, but I have not written a word. I am starting to be very, very frightened. I'm obsessed by censorship. *In Italics*, my latest work, received not a word from the press. It is the only book of its kind on ethnicity and no one spoke about it. Silence of this sort frightens me.

PV: That is what is keeping you from writing?

AD: Yes. In fact, it also affects me as a publisher.

PV: I was trying to think back. I do not think we always agreed on the role of multiculturalism, or what is *Italianità*. We did not always agree on the definition or the role of ethnicity. But, somehow, I think we came to the same place via different directions. And part of it has to do also with the fact that I am trying to figure out my own position within the so-called Italian community in North America, the community of writers.

Most writers are of a different emigrant generation than I, and therefore their interests are also different from mine. So I do not really know where I stand. My primary interest has not been in ethnicity in a strict sense, but in learning to communicate in a different language, using a different language, and extending that language beyond the boundaries of its nationalisms. I think I came to ethnicity through that door.

AD: But your position (if I remember correctly back in the 1980s) was one of being alternative. You were always anti-nationalistic.

PV: Oh, Yes. Definitely. I kept stressing it at every conference. My dialogue was not only against Canadian nationalism, but also against Italian nationalism. That is why I cannot accept all the claims rising from *Italianità*. Not only did I feel deracinated in Canada, but I felt that the reasons for my lack of roots were a result of the Italian sociocultural reality. It wasn't only Canada imposing its culture, but I felt I had been exposed to that imposition as a result of Italy having imposed its own terms on me as a child. If we agree that history has not ended, that we are a result of and live in history, how can anyone then deny their background? We must analyze why we might perceive our culture as a prison. But I have not seen anyone do that yet.

AD: A new category of writers has emerged. A new experience has grown through the years, one that we helped define. I do not think the historians were ahead of us. The historians were talking about what they knew, which was a history of people leaving one land and going to another. That is why they were saying: "We are just a passing phase." The problem was, and the problem still is that, no, this is not a passing phase. This can be a permanent and fruitful experience.

But people keep reminding me that this can be a permanent experience only if you are a nationalistic Italian or a nationalistic Canadian. This reasoning stems from a melting pot ideology on a higher scale. We are still talking melting pot. The emphasis is on culture, but those cultures that are being cross-cultured, transcultured, are expected to be strong cultures. Whereas I am saying that a culture that is *debole,* that has faded, is the most interesting in possibilities.

That is, all culture is basically an impermanent mutation. Culture, for it to be vital, should be in a weakened position. It should be in such a defeated position that it cannot negotiate with other cultures. These ideas lead me to split with the *Vice Versa* group.

PV: That's something we haven't mentioned. You are one of the founders of *Vice Versa* with Fulvio Caccia, Lamberto Tassinari, Bruno Ramirez, and Gianni Caccia. And so your parting of the ways was based on this ideological thing.

AD: Ideology started it, because they would always use the word *transculturalism* to describe what we were doing. That became the key word that Quebecois identified us with. As soon as I started criticizing the term, I became a writer in my own space, without a space. That is when the Quebecois opened doors for me. Though I was taking a position against *Vice Versa,* many writers did not fully grasp my position. It certainly did not always automatically favor a pro-Quebecois position. And as soon as nationalists found this weak link in my work, they criticized me again.

PV: They're more Quebecois nationalists than Italian nationalists.

AD: That would apply to English Canadians as well. The principal misunderstanding is that for many there is no Canadian nationalism. They are wrong. Canadian nationalism is so strong that it leaves no space for other voices to be heard. There never is a space for a different voice in English Canada. It is English Canada that pushed Quebec into territorial nationalism (which I feel it is not in essence). Quebec is more open to Others.

I am pro-French, but I am against the way the Quebecois base their identity on territory. It is a historical mistake from which they must free themselves. If the Quebecois would base themselves on culture (or ethnicity), they would probably gain more sympathy from the rest of North America. Territoriality requires decrees that often usurp individual rights.

PV: Definitely. That is the way I have always felt about Quebec, too. I always thought Quebec was a wonderful example of what could happen in a positive direction, culturally speaking, in North America.

But the nationalist phase that has grown to manipulate immigrant communities and legislate the death of their cultures has totally pushed me away from them.

AD: I feel this is a passing phase. Strangely enough, I think it is a plebeian phase versus the noble phase. What makes Quebec interesting was the fact that it was a Catholic stronghold. As soon as that stopped, around 1953, with the coming to the fore of the nationalist poets Gaston Miron and the poets Miron published at his press l'Hexagone, culture in Quebec became very territorial.

In the 1970s and 80s the language writers of Quebec were for a while anti-territorial, they were internationalizing their literary experiments. Writers like Nicole Brossard, André Roy, Jean Paul Daoust, Claude Beausoleil were going way beyond the nationalist call of duty.

They had this movement that opened wide towards the Francophonie. It was beautiful to see. I was fortunate enough to be allowed to participate in this flurry of international activity. I am still very close to these poets because they are very much into the globalization of Quebec culture. They work in groups and do much to help the world understand what Quebec is all about. I learned a lot by being with them. They were the ones who gave me the tools that I needed for what I was trying to accomplish as an Italic writer. They forced me to enlarge my reality, no longer basing my identity on Italy or Canada but as supra-nationalist subject, a non-territorial writer with a cause.

PV: We were living in two very different situations. You were living in Quebec, and I was living in the very lost Vancouver at the same time. Vancouver really only began to open up at around that time. Obviously, there were always minority groups, but they were less visible, and I knew very few Italians in Vancouver. The area where we lived was mostly Scottish and British. And when I moved to Victoria from Vancouver, it was even worse. That was like living in England. It became very frustrating for me to work in Victoria, because I could not discuss any of the issues that started to preoccupy me. I did not have anyone to discuss them with.

AD: There is a facilitator now, Smaro Kamboureli?

PV: But she was not there when I was there.

AD: She was going through the same process as we were. I met her a few years back and we spent an entire day together taping our conversation, but the tapes were lost. I like her. She is Macedonian, she comes from a country divided in three, which gives her a widened view of her own identity.

Now — there's another group that needs a lot of unification, the Greeks.

PV: In Winnipeg, this young Greek woman came to the conference. She was really excited about what we were doing, and she wanted to establish a dialogue between Italians and Greeks in Canada. She sent me an essay. It was autobiographical, talking about these issues. So apparently there is a need for our kind of activity in every minority group. Except when you really get close, all the territoriality and regionalism, what Italians call *campanilismo*, rears its head. While people are saying "we are all Italians" out of one side of their mouth, the accusations about North and South soon emerge. The Greeks have similar problems. Canadians have the same problem. If we are talking about culture free of circumscription, then we are going to get somebody screaming, "This is our real culture, not yours!"

AD: By silencing us, nationalists managed to do exactly what they wanted: they have reduced us to the status of marginal writers who are just making a lot of noise for no reason. Complainers for nothing. By systematically pushing people to the margins, mainstream culture creates a situation of antagonism which it cherishes. Every time we speak, we come out as sour grapes, when, in fact, we are trying to better our cultures.

PV: That is how one creates censorship. If you say something within or without your community, you are bound to get hit from one side or the other. In contrast to what you said about being less willing to speak openly, lately I find that I am more willing to speak. I care less and less about how it may be received. Because I figure I am already in a marginal position as a writer, people will not receive my words anyway. My speaking cannot keep people from buying my books because they do not buy them in any case.

AD: I am enchanted by what the French-language writing has enabled me to understand. It really allows desire and politics to be articulated clearly. One day, critics were being forced by distributors and bookstores to speak well about certain ethnic books that they had originally lambasted. That was amazing. The doodling was so obvious that I wrote to the editors of *Le Devoir* in Montreal complaining about how they misrepresented the entire question of ethnic writing. I was able to follow how they were able to destroy one writer one week, and then slowly change their view the next, until on the third week they were declaring the same writer the best Canadian writer of all time. We were all permitted to see how the press can turn overnight a lousy writer into the most important Canadian writer. Man, you should have seen how they had to excuse themselves all along! The worse is that they were right in the first place: the writer *was* bad.

PV: It's incredible. The power of the press to really direct culture.

AD: More than the press it is the machinery behind literature. What has happened is a gradual global swing to right-wing politics. We are under the reign of right-wing politicians at this moment. One can detect by reading reviews across the country this undeniable shift to the right. It is blatant in newspapers everywhere. In Toronto, the press is outspoken about its favor for this renewed shift to the right. Imagine headlines like "The Right-Wing Parties Should Unite" spoken by a provincial Premier as if he were speaking of pudding! It is alarming. Have people already forgotten what monstrosities right-wing politics created only fifty years ago? Today right-wing policies have the candy-flavor of money, and so they are easier to swallow. The results of these atrocious policies are nevertheless staggering. And all in the name of efficiency!

Right-wing politics has imposed a distinct type of readership which, in turn, has fostered a certain need in publishers to produce selective types of books. Slowly, from experimental and youthful writing, we have been thrown into a normative kind of narrative writing, which is totally mainstreamly dispassionate. Totally acceptable writing, commas in the proper place, dainty adjectives to express teflonic emotions (to use a Melfi term), characters that have no past, no present, no future. Writers are without history, stories with history, even when they are supposed to be about history. The most boring reproduction of simple linear narratives. You notice this trend across the world. The awful writing that is coming out is so second rate that one wonders if first-class literature ever existed. This literature in bad taste is slowly rewriting people's taste for things literary. How can people ever enjoy Guernica books in such a climate? Our books must seem, bluntly put, "bad."

PV: I find appealing what you said about being able to take advantage of the writing in Quebec, because I have always been jealous of what was going on in Montreal, what you as a writer had available. I was always very jealous, compared to what I had in Victoria and Vancouver. In Montreal, it seemed to me that you had a lot of activity with the small presses, with the journals. It just seemed so great to be there and be able to extract from one and the other, the French, the English, the Italian. That is something that always attracted me to Montreal.

AD: I was fortunate, I learned the French language so that I could participate in all that activity. I do not understand the anglos in Quebec who do not speak French. They are losing out on so much. I have a real love for that culture. I am not ashamed to say I am totally Quebecois and Canadian in my liking of literature. I am a writer because I read good Quebecois and Canadian books.

I grew up reading everything that was going on in Canada. The writers I loved first come from Canada. So it hurts like hell to be tossed aside since I feel that my job is to promote Canadian and Quebecois culture. But there is so much hurt one can take. When I translated Philippe Haeck whom I consider the most important living Canadian writer, not a word was said about his work. He is as important and as deep seated in culture as Donald Hall is in the U.S.A. I hear in Donald Hall Philippe Haeck's voice and vice versa. Leonard Cohen, Marshall McLuhan, John Buell, Gwendolyn MacEwen, Margaret Atwood, John Newlove, Tonino Caticchio with his popular songs, I mean, I loved them all. Then you get into prose writing.

Prose writing, I found in general, lacking in passion. They obviously never read Elizabeth Smart or James Baldwin, your favorite writers. I must tell you, I never really liked much of the prose writing in Canada, because I always thought it was imitative of what was good in other forms. It is only recently that I discovered fine prose writers; I like Barry Callaghan, Matt Cohen, and Fernard Ouellette.

PV: I think English Canadian prose, to generalize greatly, is very much influenced by British prose, no matter who writes it. I find it quite un-interesting.

AD: You can read New Zealand writers, Australian and South African writers and soon you notice their writing styles are different. There is an urgency that should be necessary but that is not always there. There is no urgency in much of English Canadian prose. The most important writing being done in North America is done in memoirs. I love memoirs. That is why I like reading essays, because essays are very memoir-ish.

For instance, *Being Digital* by Nicholas Negroponte is like reading a memoir. Roland Barthes is still my favorite prose writer. How to talk about philosophy, technology, and still manage to talk about oneself? It is very much like poetry, but less complicated, because poetry is very complicated.

The best writing is achieved when each text refers back to life. My concept of essentialism comes from this dual relationship of all writing — a culturally knowledgeable text bathing in a memoir.

PV: Some denounce the autobiography.

AD: I love autobiographies. *Le récit,* the French call it. This is about a particular moment in your life that you want to talk about. And it can even be invented!

PV: Like the ones by Annie Ernaux.

AD: You're right. You're right.

PV: It's called *Une femme (A Woman)* . . .

AD: That stuff is beautiful. That type of writing is really moving. Short. Precise. Extremely powerful emotionally. Well written. You cannot lie in a memoir. Someone once told me that in a memoir each sentence has to be real all the time. He is right. There is a difference on the formal level between truth and reality. Whether the text is invented or not, the memoir has to talk about truth. It has to be real. That realness is what makes the reader want to continue reading. In a memoir, as soon as you falsify something, the text flops. You close the book.

I really enjoyed Penny Petrone's book, *Breaking the Mould*. It got no reviews, and she was totally hurt by the critical silence. Here is a woman who, an important scholar of native cultures, is suddenly ostracized when she comes out with a book about being Italian. No one has spoken about that book. This critical darkness proves that certain autobiographical themes are more acceptable than others.

PV: Canadians do not want to face certain facts. There are certain steps that you have to take towards a criticism of our position. We keep stepping back from it, because the ideas are threatening.

The writer/publisher business

PV: Usually, a writer approaches a publisher because he or she is interested in the sort of work that the publisher does, in the direction taken by the press. Not just because you do not know where the hell to send it.

AD:. There are plenty of chances for people to meet me in Toronto. They can actually come to our launchings and our readings. They can even write to me. I wrote to writers I loved. I remember the first time I bought a book by Philippe Haeck in 1974. I wrote to him and said, "I love your work." We don't have that in the community. We're not a book people. People write to me saying, "Well, Nino made it big. I want to make it big, too."

PV: You have made yourself very available. Maybe too available. It becomes too easy in the sense that you are now taken for granted. "I'll send him a manuscript. He'll do it." That does away with people realizing how tough it is to get a publisher. It is not easy. You have done it for a lot of writers. You have published a lot of writers' first books. Often on their first try. They did not have to go any further, because you were there, and you provided a service. You had a specific direction that you had decided on, so if they came to you, you were available.

Before I found you, I sent out work to so many presses. I was not going to send it out to anybody else. I had given up. I really mean a lot of presses. So I was turned down by all of these publishers. I did not genuinely expect to be accepted because I knew the type of work they had been publishing and what they were interested in.

I knew one of the editors for a British Columbia press. He shaped that press editorially, and it was very obvious. Maybe too obvious. That is in fact the job of an editor or a mentor such as he was and is still. But in some cases the editorial choices are based so much on themes and subject matter and style that it all becomes rather predictable and insipid. I stopped picking up that press's books because I knew what to expect. It becomes harmful for writers, who get locked into a precise mode of expression by a press. There is no room for innovation.

AD: When I sent in my manuscripts, they were always turned down. They always answered back, saying, "Where do you fit in? If you want me to publish your work, where do you fit in?" I had to begin to do my homework. "Where do you fit in? Why should I publish your work? Why do you want to be published by us?" I was friends with the editors of many presses, and they still turned my works down because they were not the press for me. I would drink with the editors and writers every night, and they still turned me down. "You don't belong in this movement. We love you but you're not part of this."

PV: Those presses emerged with movements in mind. I don't disagree with that, but I do think that it is different from dictating content and form based on aesthetics.

AD: That's right. The people in charge were always very honest with me. They could have destroyed me. They never did. One day, Jacques Lanctôt stopped me and said: "I think I'm the publisher you're looking for." I stayed with him until he sold his press to a large press which I did not care for.

PV: You notice by who comes to your readings, in whatever city you are, who is interested in your work. By who comes and, mostly, by who does not come to your readings. It is not a matter of expecting everyone to show up every time. But I have always been very supportive of writers, no matter what style they write in. I always try to support them. I go to a lot of the readings, mostly just to be supportive. But after you go to three or four readings by one person and this person does not ever come to yours, then it is time to cut the line. It is part of the larger working ethic of the profession. Try to show respect for what people do.

AD: People think you are a radical writer.

PV: My sort of writing does not fit into many editors' idea of what we should be writing. When I send in work for an anthology it is sent back with a critique telling me how I should be writing, how I should be more autobiographical, be truer to my heritage and all that shit. It bothers me when people tell me what I should be writing, because they want me to fit into their mold. This is our reality. I am part of that reality. It is like institutionalized multiculturalism in Canada. If you do not like it, fine. That is all you have to say. Do not tell me what I should be writing. I know that's what it comes to. This idea they have that I am a post-modernist, they do not even know what the word means. It is a put-down of sorts, actually. I fight it sometimes if I am in the mood, and I do not ever expect to be invited twice to the same place.

There is an agenda here. They have to present us in a certain manner, and if it does not fit into that mold, why should they even think about me. It is not their view of literature. If you do not present your own view of things, these things do not exist.

AD: I imagine your position is painful, and it is painful because . . .

PV: When I edit something, I worry that I might be doing it from my own sense of poetics. I try to base my editing and decisions on the quality of the poetry, and not the style or what it is about. If it is good poetry, it is good poetry. A poet should have a voice. But I think, from the other side, it does not quite work that way. And the inequality is painful. I have written a lot, but very few have ever said anything about it.

If we are doing an anthology of Italian Canadian writers, then all the styles deserve to be included. One might deal with the issues differently.

AD: Those words lead us to the main issue, which is . . . What makes us who we are? People want to pigeon hole us; the critics and even we wish for a pragmatic reality. We are determined by our careers. We are writers. We should be proud to have this ability to communicate. Where the meeting of the minds becomes really a meeting of the minds and styles, and not a meeting of dramatics.

PV: I was not born in Canada, and did not start to learn English right away. It came as a process. So the reader should have to go through that same process. One day I should write a little poem about my social studies teacher insisting that Rome was in Campania. I remember saying in my very bad English: "I'm from Naples. Naples is in Campania. Rome is in Lazio." But the guy insisted, "No, you're wrong." So I showed him on the map in the classroom. It became a matter of claiming voice and history. He didn't like it.

But I have no use for those funny, little stories. To me it does not amount to an experience. All I would be telling you is a story. It is something that I did not initiate. I want to be the initiator of my stories.

AD: In these stories, we end up being victims.

PV: We are constantly reacting to these situations. Someone initiates, someone calls you a "dago guinea," and you react. It is all about becoming the historian of one's own life.

AD: I always end my readings with the poem "Italia mia amore." I could have ended the poem with a message filled with hatred, a call for war. Instead I chose to summon love. I am not going to deal with social issues as a victim.

PV: The way that others want us to.

AD: I am going to deal with you in a totally different way. I will give you my love and see how you react to that. Then *you* have got the problem, not I. Then it becomes your story and not my story.

PV: Pier Paolo Pasolini has a line that I quote in *The Posthumous Poet*. Something about confronting the enemy with the force and the violence of love. He wrote about the violence of love. That way, you have the upper hand. You take the initiative. You not only react to what they are saying, but you turn it around, and you say something yourself, that is based within yourself. You manipulate the material.

AD: And then it becomes a legal matter. After you have reacted out of love and you still get beaten on, then you take them to court. We are not there yet.

PV: We need to act on some organized level. It is about us. We have to be activists. We really have to be that. We have not done that yet. We have just started.

San Diego, June 15-17, 1996.

Achevé d'imprimer en octobre 1998 chez

à Boucherville, Québec